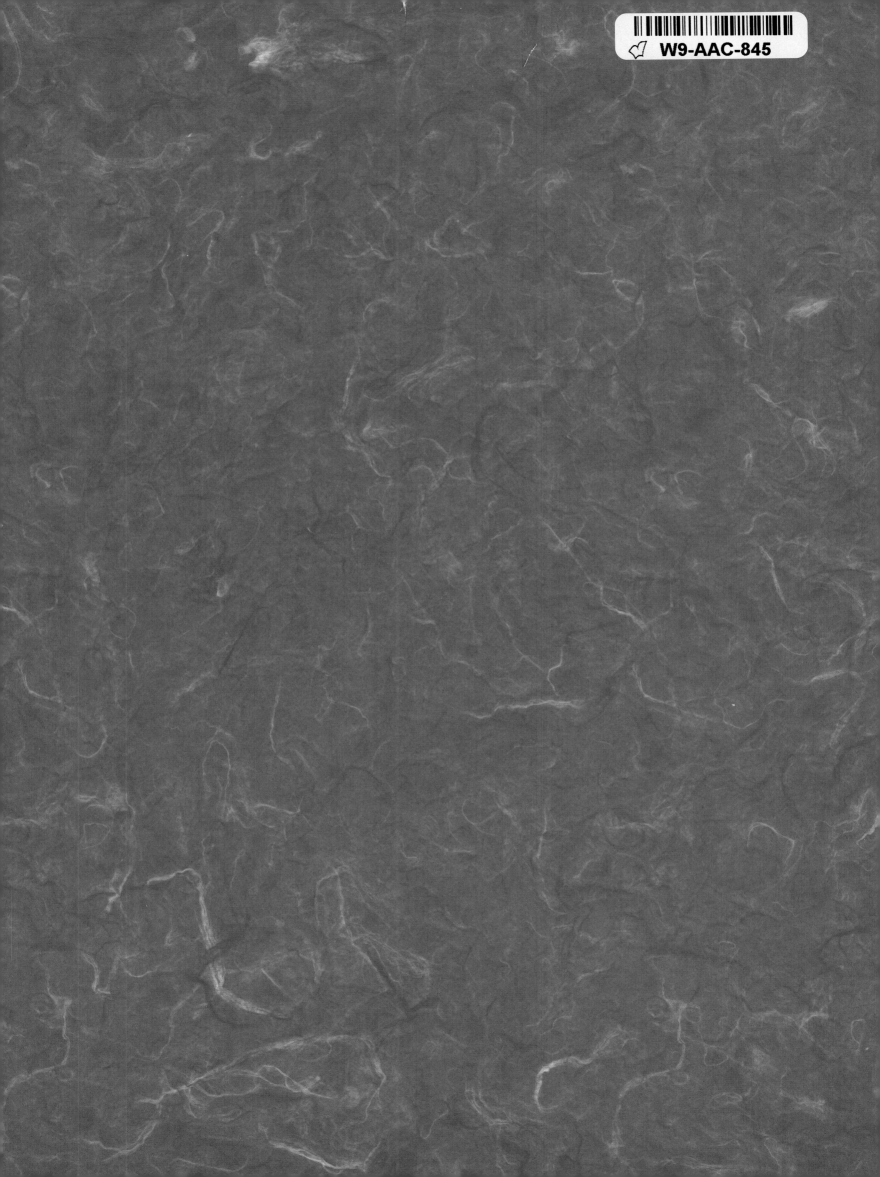

RICHMOND

Dear Reader,

Please accept this unique special edition book, **Hong Kong Dawn of a New Dynasty** with the compliments and best wishes of Richmond Asset Management.

Richmond has been established in Hong Kong since 1992. While serving clients worldwide, we have a strong commitment to business in the Asian-Pacific region, with an associated office in Perth, Western Australia and plans for further expansion within Asia in the future.

As you know we at Richmond provide specialised investment services for investors seeking a **personalised** and **innovative** approach to investment.

Above all we believe that **timing is the key** to the long term preservation and creation of wealth and this is demonstrated by our use of up-to-the-minute research and a sophisticated management system.

Finally, we believe **flexibility** is important and our services are designed to be tailored to suit individual requirements and circumstances. Our services include cash management, investment through offshore bonds and fund timing for unit trusts and multi-currency mortgages.

We hope you will enjoy this beautiful book and look forward to continuing to service your investment needs for many years to come.

With best regards,

Graham Bibby

Graham Bibby
Managing Director

RICHMOND ASSET MANAGEMENT LIMITED

SUITE 801, 8/F, CRE BUILDING, 303 HENNESSY ROAD, HONG KONG TEL: (852) 2827 5138 FAX: (852) 2596 0024 EMAIL: RAMHK@NETVIGATOR.COM

BAYON PUBLISHING (H.K.) LTD.

5/F Yee Hing Loong Building
151 Hollywood Rd.
Central, Hong Kong.

Telephone: (852) 2543-9557 Fax: (852) 2543-8907

Mark Presley

Publishers Chris Coombes   Deborah Scully   Mike Cheek   Mark Burgio

Designer Harry Llufrio

Colour Separation Universal Colour Scanning Limited

Printed by Green Production Group in Hong Kong

Contents

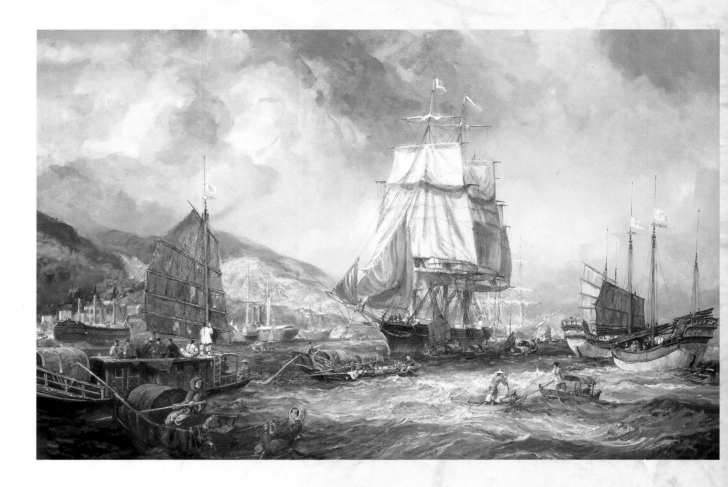

INTRODUCTION

Nature has a knack of providing a level of quality that human endeavor strives to reach but seldom matches. If one was to choose a place to locate a harbour positioned as strategically and so naturally protected as Hong Kong, the location of 114° 10'E and 22° 15'N would be hard to match. The British Foreign Secretary, Lord Palmerston, in 1841 was heard to scoff "Hong Kong is nothing more than a barren rock." Surely the underestimation of the 19th century, as today Hong Kong stands as the success story of the Orient.

On June 30th, 1997 at midnight, the whole world turned up or tuned in to see if this success story was set to continue. The British flag was lowered and the new Hong Kong Bauhinia flag was unfurled along with the red and gold stars of the People's Republic of China. We were treated to a spectacular array of displays, dignitaries, discussions and decisions. A chapter in history had been written, and Hong Kong still glowed as the pearl of the Orient. Tens of thousands of journalists reported the story to every corner of the globe. There was barely a living person who did not have an opinion about the future of this region. The television set became a high-tec crystal ball. Through the rain the people of Hong Kong looked on with dignity. A new era had started and all the worries and the fears of the last ten years were lost in the start of a bold new beginning. Just as quickly as our guests had arrived they were gone. Everyone had moved onto the next story and the population of this great city kept doing what they do best - succeeding.

*H*ong Kong, when translated into English, means Fragrant Harbour, a name that might seem a little ironic today. It is one of the busiest ports in the world due to its strategic position in Asia, but in relative terms it is still young as a commercial port. It sits on the coast of China's Guangdong province and is strategically placed at the mouth of the Pearl River, 130 kilometres southeast of Guangzhou. It lies in the tropics, just a few degrees south of the Tropic of Cancer. Hong Kong is an Archipelago of over 200 solid rock islands that nestle in the South China Sea. Although the region was ceded to Britain over 150 years ago it is undoubtedly a part of China. This undeniable asset of its character is one of the main reasons why it is an economic colossus of the Asian region.

The early residents of the region consisted of three different groups of Southern Chinese. The warm South China Seas provided an ample stock of fish for the Tanka and Hoklo Fisherfolk. It seems that they existed in this region since Neolithic times and even today the fishing boats are a regular part of the local scenery. The land was tilled by Hakka Farmers who can still be seen working the paddy fields, conspicuous in their black clothes and their elaborate wide-brimmed hats. The small bays and harbours also offered shelter to pirates who patrolled the South China Sea, looking for unsuspecting traders who sailed down from the Northern Chinese ports bound for the Indies. However it was not until the mid-18th century that the region started to grow as a port as a result of the overspill of the East India Company, and it was not governments that made the first links between China and Britain, but rather the imagination of industrious traders.

The region became useful to the Chinese traders of the Middle Kingdom with the expansion of the spice trade between Europe and the East Indies. The East India Company developed a trading monopoly with the local businessmen whom were known as *co-hong* merchants. *Hong* is the Chinese word for a trade which qualified such commodities as herbal tea, a massive business at that time. This differentiated them from the normal Chinese traders or *hongs* who each had their own particular lines of business. Many of the *co-hong* traders made huge fortunes at this time and their offspring are some of the wealthiest families in Hong Kong today.

But with success comes greed and the arrival of opium from India caused grave concern to the Imperial Government which made it illegal. However the trade did not stop and the increase of smuggling of opium started to strip the Middle Kingdom of its wealth of silver, used to pay for this addictive commodity. It was estimated in the book *The Opium War* that from 1821 to 1840 one fifth of the total wealth of silver in China was lost to fund this illegal smuggling. At this time the Qing Dynasty became increasingly concerned about the effects of opium use on the once hard working population. They became lazy and un-reliable and took easily to the addictive, intoxicating effect of the drug. This, combined with the drain on the silver wealth, required action.

An official from Hunan and Hupeh provinces was appointed. His name was Lin Tse-hsu. Lin had had a successful term as governor of Hunan and Hupeh and more or less personally removed opium from the daily lives of the population of these regions.

Commissioner Lin arrived in Canton in March 1839 and immediately outlawed the importation of opium. Large quantities were seized from the local and foreign merchants and burnt. The traders were then obliged to sign a treaty undertaking never to import the drug again. Charles Elliott, Chief British Trade Superintendent, ordered the British traders not to agree to such an undertaking.

Lin immediately ordered the end of Sino-British trade and closed Canton to the British Merchants. So began the first Opium War.

Sadly for the Chinese, Lin was the only leader in the region able to defend Canton. The other cities along the coast fell one by one to the British. The Imperial Government eventually was forced to remove Lin from his post and make the peace. The Island of Hong Kong was ceded to Britain in 1841 to the then Superintendent of Trade, Captain Charles Elliot RN, who was the first administrator of the Colony. The Treaty of Nankin in 1842 finally ended the two year war and heavy fines were imposed upon the Chinese. This enabled the British to hold a strategic trading port in the region, ruled by a British administration, with the objective to conduct trade with China.

On the sixth of January 1842 Sir Henry Pottinger, Hong Kong's first Governor, declared Hong Kong a free port. This bold move was the catalyst needed to improve the development of trade on an ever increasing scale. It is also a policy that still remains today and many people consider it to be the main reason for the continued success of this region.

However this did nothing to contain the cross border wrangling between the British and the Chinese. Hong Kong became notorious for harbouring China's political dissidents and also had a constant battle on its hands as it tried to contain China's attempts to mobilise Hong Kong patriots in its tussles against the British. Such matters as the poisoned loaves incident, where Chinese patriots put arsenic into the bread eaten by the expatriate community, was one of many such incidents. All was not well as the end of the nineteenth century approached; stocks plummeted, property prices slumped and houses stood empty as a surplus of accommodation became a problem.

However, recession is not part of the nature of this region and in 1898, the Hongkong and Shanghai Banking Corporation and Jardine Matheson & Co. formed the British and Chinese Corporation, to

provide the capital needed to service any concessions granted to the region from China. In 1898 the Canton to Kowloon Railway was constructed. In the same year Britain was able to extract a 99 year lease out of China for 350 square miles of land north of the Kowloon peninsular known as the New Territories.

Kowloon, the land north of Hong Kong Island, was part of the Chinese mainland. Kowloon, means nine Dragons and refers to the nine hills that run from east to west from the New Territories to Tsim Sha Tsui. It was essential for the further development of Hong Kong that this land was under British control, as it was a buffer between Hong Kong and mainland China. It was also the main cause for the reunification of Hong Kong with China. The end of the lease was the catalyst for the handover, but in today's modern world Colonial power is regarded as an out-dated form of Government.

From 1898 onwards China went through the dramas of civil war and unrest. Hong Kong became a haven for thousands of Chinese people who looked to the foreign government for refuge from the unrest that occurred in China at that time. By 1937, Hong Kong's population passed the one million mark and by 1941, prior to the Japanese occupation, the population had reached a staggering figure - 1,639,000 people.

At this time Japan emerged as a world power and this, combined with the demise of free trade, became significant in the development of the region. Japan was dominating the region with an aggressive commercial policy and was becoming alarmingly aggressive on a military front as well. Japanese products were starting to flood the market and the competition caused Britain to give up the principle of free trade, a policy that had worked for 100 years. It did however maintain the free port status that was to prove crucial to the region. During this time the situation in China started to become more and more complicated. Kuomintang government at that time had a firm grip on the development of trade in the region proposing the removal of trading restrictions with Britain, the United States, Japan and France. Sadly this position of strength could not last and soon mainland China was plunged into civil war.

This had a profound effect on the balance of trade in the region as China looked to import more and more goods from Hong Kong. This contrasted dramatically with the decline of exports due to the internal conflicts. The relations with China and Japan deteriorated to such an extent that war became inevitable and Hong Kong became drawn into the conflict. The Japanese attacked and captured Hong Kong in December 1941 and controlled the region for three years and eight months. Their occupation was regarded by many as the worst time the region has ever undergone and their cruel and callous treatment of civilians in Hong Kong is well documented. It was with a huge sigh of relief that Rear Admiral C. J. Harcourt received the official surrender of the Japanese Army in 1945 and everyone in Hong Kong hoped that life would be back to normal as soon as possible. The War had

been an inconvenient distraction from what the local people liked to do best, work and achieve. But from the aftermath of the war a new future without Colonial rulers was to begin. The British Empire was to be dismantled and autonomy for Hong Kong became a realistic option.

The post war Governor at that time was Sir Mark Young who tried to incorporate a new franchise for the election of a Municipal Council. This was to be partially made up of elected locals who would chart the development of the territory. This plan was never to come into action as the Mao Tse-tung's People's Liberation Army was transforming China and creating a new type of mass migration to Hong Kong. Young's policies were never realised as the problem of an exodus of refugees arrived in Kowloon. The population of this little corner of China swelled from 1,600,000 people in 1946 to a staggering 2,500,000 at the end of 1956. Hong Kong became swamped with squatter towns as the new arrivals made the best of the limited space, putting all the infrastructure of the already crowded city under immense strain.

The Korean war was to follow and once again the region strained at the restrictions made on China by the Americans. However the industry of the people in the region enabled a quick and efficient restructure of the working ethic. Hong Kong quickly built factories and used the recent influx of migrants from China to man their new industrial ideals. China was undergoing massive changes with the Great Leap Forward and was beginning to learn the price of such radical change with famine and starvation. Many of the recent arrivals in Hong Kong tried to stave off the inevitable hardships of their families in China by sending food and clothes to the many who suffered in this troubled time. Many disgruntled, starving Chinese marched to Hong Kong to look for a new beginning as the poverty and starvation in areas such as Canton grew. This became compounded a few years later by the Cultural Revolution in 1966 which again caused a mass migration to this tiny island.

It says a great deal about the Chinese character that throughout the 1960's, Hong Kong was consolidating its position as a major industrial region. The large quantity of new workers who were eager to develop the new industrialised region were proving invaluable. The local businessmen were making their own businesses and consolidating their hold in this new commercial region. The big Hongs such as Swire and Jardine's were still strong, but a new breed of local businessman was also flourishing using the ever buoyant economy to fuel their success.

The stock market was becoming a Cantonese trading floor as, prior to this, the British had dealt in English. This enabled speculators to raise large quantities of money for developments. The 1970's also saw the use of technology in the markets and this helped to develop a new type of world trade. A trade that offered a fantastic chance for Hong Kong to be the Asian linchpin with its already highly organised infrastructure. It was therefore inevitable that Hong Kong should become a financial centre of Asia.

the unprecedented success of this territory. The other crucial factor was the proximity of the motherland and all the untapped potential it held. In the year 1978 Hong Kong was prepared for the changes that were taking place in China with the return of Deng Xiaoping and the new 'Open Door Policy'. Unlike his predecessor, Mao, he believed in a prosperous business future for China with the emphasis taken away from the military and placed on economic reform. Businessmen latched onto this quickly and moved their manufacturing facilities to South China while keeping the administration of these facilities in Hong Kong. The trade balance, already relatively high, increased by thousands of percentages over the next fifteen years and the successful development of the region continued into the mega city it is today.

The only other thing that rocked the foundations of Hong Kong was the agreement between Deng Xiaoping and Margaret Thatcher in 1984, the much publicised Joint Sino-British Declaration. This concluded that when the lease of the New Territory was up on June 30th 1997, the territory would return to the motherland in its entirety. Many at this time, predicted the demise of this great city with the arrival of the administration of the mainland Chinese, however Deng Xiaoping concocted a policy of 'one country, two systems' to harness the potential benefits of working closely with the mainland. Opinions were mixed with regard to this policy and at first their was some negativity towards this concept. But all those who predicted doom and gloom for Hong Kong have had to reassess their position as the region has gone on from strength to strength.

The handover of Sovereignty of Hong Kong to China and all the predictions for this region seem a distant memory. It seems that the entire media circus descended on Hong Kong with a pre-conceived notion that this was to be the end of the economic miracle. A few months have passed and the economic situation in the region has never been better. The economy is holding firm in comparison to some of the other Asian Tigers, providing a stable base for further growth. The new SAR Government is working hard and well for the future of the people in this region and the prospects of increased links with China are undoubtedly beneficial. Mr Tung Chee-hwa's firm yet reasonable working style as the new Chief Executive has proved to be a breath of fresh air as he has a crucial role to follow. His experiences on an international scale can only help the region to prosper. His defined understanding of the running of both the Chinese and western culture can only benefit both sides. However it is the people of Hong Kong who hold the key to the future of the region.

Hong Kong is not a city that has been built up over hundreds of years, but rather over a period of barely 200 years. It has been built around the mutual understanding of traders from the East and the West. This and this alone will decide the future of this amazing region as the continuation of successful trade will be the bench-mark for a successful future. The great leaps that China has made over the last twenty years will hopefully lead Hong Kong into the new millennium as the international marketplace of this vibrant region.

The key to the continued success of Hong Kong must remain as the individuality of the people who inhabit this region. Once they lose their ability to be a distinctive type of Asian businessman the region will lose its uniqueness. Hong Kong was built on trade and should maintain its status as a free port. The combination of local Chinese inhabitants and the international businessmen who set up their representative offices here, is also crucial for both parties. China has emerged from the nineteenth century as the leading country in this booming Asian region. If the people of Hong Kong can harness this potential the future for this vibrant city remains prosperous. The infrastructure is in place for the leap into the new millennium and the people of Hong Kong are ready to make that leap. The region has returned to the motherland and we have at last entered the 'Dawn of a New Dynasty'.

大興土木

BUILDING
A CITY

The world's longest suspension bridge, carrying both road and rail traffic, was inaugurated in May 1997 with a marathon race and a spectacular fireworks display.

MARTIN BUCKLEY

MARTIN BUCKLEY

The Tsing Ma Bridge is a formidable sight. This link with the future is more than 200 metres high.

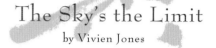

The Sky's the Limit
by Vivien Jones

In a mere century and a half, the world has witnessed Hong Kong's transformation from a cluster of sleepy fishing villages into one of the most dynamic and prosperous metropolises on the planet. The oft-dubbed 'barren rock' has triumphed through a mix of hard work, ingenuity and a liberal dose of what the Chinese call *jup sang* (which literally means to 'grasp life'). Concentrated in less than 1,100 square kilometres with few natural resources to recommend it, Hong Kong is now the freest economy in the world and a leading international trade and finance centre. Few who visit fail to be astonished by what they see.

The first glimpse of Hong Kong island across the crowded harbour, steely skyscrapers clinging to the waters edge, is enough to confirm this city's dynamic reputation. The throb of industry and energy is almost palpable. It is hard to imagine that one misguided colonist dismissed the place as producing nothing, not leading to any place.

MARTIN BUCKLEY

PETER DANFORD

DAVE PARKER

MAIRI SEMPLE

Others were a sight more perspicacious. Sir Henry Pottinger soon predicted that Hong Kong would become a vast emporium of wealth and the key was the harbour, from which *Heung Gong* took its name. One of the world's finest deep water ports, it was this natural asset that first alerted the British to Hong Kong's potential as a trading enclave. Just as Kong's first inhabitants relied on the sea for their living, so have successive generations forged wealth from it.

Today the harbour remains a hub of Hong Kong's activities. Where elegant clipper ships bearing opium and tea once sailed, massive container ships and luxury liners now cruise. Stalagmite skyscrapers, glinting on the waterfront, have replaced the Victorian godowns and fishing villages of old.

More than 100 ships of every size and rig, from every corner of the globe, arrive through the choppy swell each day. Ferries to the outlying islands bear commuters and day-trippers west. Hydrofoils and hovercraft make for Macau and China. Luxury junks and sleek power boats take revellers out for a day in the sun. Police launches patrol the waters. Sampans and fishing boats dart in and out, ferrying their cargo to land. Cutting through this congestion, the famed Star Ferry carries 96,000 passengers every day on a five minute voyage that must rate as one of the most exciting in the world. More than two-thirds of Hong Kong's total area is covered by water, so taking to the sea has always been part of life.

Above: *Bamboo is a cost-effective, environmentally safe material used everywhere in Hong Kong.*

Above: *The last visible bricks of the old Hong Kong Hilton Hotel. This popular hotel has had to make way for a new and grander structure.*

The land mass of
Hong Kong is
increasing. Land
reclamation has
become a common
sight throughout
the region.

This instrument is used by Fung Shui experts who confirm the strategic positioning as an essential criteria for new successful buildings.

The futuristic looking blue structures are air vents for the underground harbour tunnel. This is another addition to the infrastructure of the region linking the new airport directly to Hong Kong Island.

The Airport Core Programme on Lantau Island is a case in point. The 1,248 hectare airport platform on the northern coast was created by levelling the neighbouring islands of Chek Lap Kok and Lam Chau into the sea at a cost of more than US$1 billion. At one point, 75 per cent of the world's deep water dredging equipment was in use on this, the worlds largest construction site. Beside the airport and railway, the programme incorporates five road projects, including 20 miles of tunnels and expressways, two reclamations of land and the construction, from scratch, of a new town. This support community, the first to be built on an outlying island and the ninth in Hong Kong, is expected to grow from an initial population of 20,000 people to ten times that number by 2011.

The new airport is due to open in April 1998 and will undoubtedly relieve congestion on Kai Tak's single runway which currently serves the busiest international cargo airport in the world and the third busiest in terms of passengers. For while Hong Kong's new airport at Chek Lap Kok may not be able to offer the white-knuckle landing approach that has made Kai Tak famous, it will be able to process 35 million passengers and three million tonnes of cargo each year. Ultimately, the airport, which cost in excess of US$20 billion, is expected to handle 87 million passengers and nine million tonnes of cargo a year. Linking this massive development with the Kowloon peninsula are three bridges: the double-deck Lantau Link; the Tsing Ma Bridge, the world's longest cable-suspension bridge; and the Kap Shui Mun Bridge, all of which will carry passengers by car and rail to Lantau and back. The railway, built specifically to serve the airport, will transport travellers from Central in just 23 minutes.

Hong Kong's new airport at Chek Lap Kok. Contractors moved 10 tonnes of material every second for 31 months to create an airport from the 302 hectare island.

A Different Type of Infrastructure

This dependency on the sea and the trade that it brought with it has built in Hong Kong the busiest container port in the world. Kwai Chung, the only privately owned and developed port in the world, deals with the cargo of 37,000 ships arriving each year. Ninety per cent of Hong Kong's trade tonnage passes through here, much of it on its way north to China, Hong Kong's largest trading partner. Plans underway to build a ninth port on the northeast side of Lantau will add more than 2.6 million TEUs (Twenty-foot Equivalent Units) to the port's annual capacity. Expected to be completed early next century, it is one of the largest civil engineering projects anywhere in the world and will double existing facilities.

Such ambitious construction is a way of life in Hong Kong. The pounding of jackhammers and pile drivers is an ever-present soundtrack for Hong Kong's residents. 'Almost nothing seems built to last', remarked author Jan Morris, and indeed it seems that no sooner does one new skyscraper shoot up than another is torn down to start the process anew. An empty building site gives way to a tower of bamboo scaffolding which in its turn is torn away to reveal another gleaming skyscraper. Reclamation projects and a voracious appetite for new buildings prompted the *South China Morning Post* to ask: 'Will Hong Kong Ever Be Finished?' In West Kowloon, reclamation increased the size of the peninsula by a third - with so little land of its own, a great deal of the land that Hong Kong has today has been claimed from the South China seas.

The Queen Elizabeth II awaits Hong Kong's last departing Civil Servants for their return voyage to Britain . In the foreground the new Convention and Exhibition Centre nears its completion.

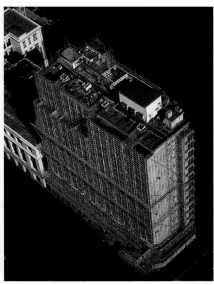

Construction workers are seen scrambling up the sides of skyscrapers upon what might seem quite a rudimentary structure, but which is actually safer than steel.

MAIRI SEMPLE

MAIRI SEMPLE

MAIRI SEMPLE

These majestic titans are the creations of some of the most famous architects in the world.

MAIRI SEMPLE

MAIRI SEMPLE

*The inimitable
architecture of
Central creates a
stunning palette of
lines and glass.
Reflections of
buildings shimmer
in the lights of day
or evening.*

Building in Hong Kong has proliferated at a rate which reflects its economic growth. High rise apartments are a notable aspect of Hong Kong's urbanised life-style.

MAIRI SEMPLE

DAVE PANKER

大興土木

Some of the older buildings, such as Government House present a stark contrast to the architect I.M. Pei's backdrop of the Bank of China Building.

Few places in the world can boast to have done so much with so little. By necessity, Hong Kong became an island of traders, bartering for what they lacked with that which they had in abundance: energy and expertise. This lack of natural resources has made Hong Kong the most trade-dependent economy in the world, worth an estimated US$376 billion in 1996. Since 1978 Hong Kong has been the main world port for China - more than a third of all trade is conducted with the mainland and ninety per cent of all re-exports are destined for there also. Such is Hong Kong's relationship with China that in mid-1997, demand on the stock market for one Red Chip firm - so-called because of their China connections - outstripped supply by 700 times.

Above: *CITIC Tower, one of the fastest buildings erected in Hong Kong had the best view of the handover ceremonies.*

Dolphins along with the Bauhinia flower have become the symbol of the new Hong Kong.

Top: *A panoramic view of Central and Wan Chai from Causeway Bay.*

Above: *The old KCR clock tower at the tip of the Kowloon peninsula still stands boldly against the skyline of the Cultural Centre at Tsim Sha Tsui.*

Right: *The Hongkong and Shanghai Bank Building.*

Right: *Central Plaza glowing in the evening sunset surpasses the Bank of China by four stories and today is still the tallest.*

Above: *The new Peak Tower is another outstanding example of the modern architecture that prevails in Hong Kong.*

Above: *Hong Kong's banks are pioneers in aesthetically pleasing architecture.*

日理萬機

HONG KONG
AT WORK

PETER DANFORD

*More than three million
people make up the SAR's
total labour force, the
majority of whom are
employed in the service
sector which contributes
significantly to
Hong Kong's financial
stability. Hence Hong
Kong's nickname as one of
the "little dragons" of Asia.*

Where does it all come from?

by Timothy Shepherd

The Stock Exchange is the inner hive of activity. It is where business gurus convene to make serious decisions.

MAIRI SEMPLE

Hong Kong is famous for its work ethic. There are some who would say that the very nature of Hong Kong - its essence - can be found in its work.

People spend seemingly endless hours toiling in great financial brokerages which sprang up years ago, and which have now come to dominate the Asia-Pacific region. You also see them in dai pai dongs, open almost around the clock - where a handful of cooks labour mightily - perhaps feeding these same late night financiers who may stop off for a bowl of noodles on their way home. You see them on the ocean, where fishermen - the first Hong Kong workers - are still there, still taking their boats out to sea and still reaping a harvest from waters incalculably more busy these days than ever before.

Whatever the job, whatever the hours, there is no disputing the fact that Hong Kong works. It would be a good campaign slogan, if one was ever needed for Hong Kong itself.

And yet to feel that Hong Kong's essence is in its work is really only part of the picture. For it is not so much the fact that there is a great deal of work done here, or that people work particularly hard, that captures Hong Kong's essential meaning. Rather it is the way the work is accomplished that is telling.

There are very few places on earth where you feel that anything is possible. There are fewer still that project this feeling so strongly that those who visit, as well as those who live here, are transformed by it. Like a scent carried on a warm spring morning, this feeling comes from a spirit that simply exudes from a place.

In New York, the spirit is dynamic and powerful. In London, the spirit is wonderfully eccentric, with the requisite nods to creativity and civility. In Paris, it is stylish, languid and sensual. Hong Kong's genius is its spirit of entrepreneurialism. The celebration of the power of the individual - through work - to create, to build, to hope and to dream. It is this spirit that represents the very nature of Hong Kong - not the work itself - but the utter belief in the possibility of bettering oneself and the willingness to rely on oneself to provide this status, that puts Hong Kong in a league of cities from whom the world has much to learn.

The dealing room at ING Barings reflects the intensity and fervour of trading in Hong Kong.

All the clichés are true: Hong Kong is a beehive of activity, a bustling, slightly manic place. But behind all this action - all this work - are people celebrating the power of the individual. That is the true work of Hong Kong and it is very much a work in progress.

Hong Kong is in the top ten of the world's trading entities by value. Throughout the year Hong Kong is host to some of the largest trading fairs in all of Asia.

MAIRI SEMPLE

Work and Play - and Work Some More

What is it actually like to work in Hong Kong? Besides it being hectic, fast-paced, exciting and crazy, it is actually quite normal.

Most people in Hong Kong live in tall blocks of flats, particularly in Kowloon and the new towns of the New Territories, like Shatin and Tsuen Mun, that were built in the 1970's and 1980's. The work day begins as people pour out of these buildings to queue for an army of mini-buses, taxis or underground trains which take the masses of people to the industrial and office areas of Kowloon and Hong Kong Island. In contrast to this early morning bustle of workers, it is common at this time of day to see older men "walking" their pet birds and other people quietly practising tai chi in the small parks often found in the huge housing estates.

Work hours are generally longer than in most other places. People in Hong Kong think nothing of working 10, 12 even 14 hour days. The work day often starts later at 9:30 or even 10:00 in the morning, but many people are still on the job at 9:00 at night. Quite a few Hong Kong people have more than one job, or else they work at their day job and then hurry home to help out in a family shop, *dai pai dong* or restaurant. Yet still the convention for most people is to work on Saturday mornings. The five and a half day working week is standard, and people who work less are considered to have received a perk.

PAUL HILTON

MoneyWorld Asia is one of the newest additions to the fast growing number of successful events.

Unlike most places, the rush to get away is not on a Friday afternoon, but Saturday at 1:00 pm. On the stroke of 1:00 a mass exodus occurs from offices and factories, often for the shopping malls or, because it is Saturday, the horse races. The experience of working in Hong Kong is a good one for most people. Wages are high, taxes are low and the possibilities to get ahead are almost endless. Upward mobility is celebrated in Hong Kong with the annual ritual of receiving a Chinese New Year's bonus of an extra month or two's pay and then promptly leaving one job for a better one. It is estimated that one in five Hong Kong employees switches jobs every year. Every Saturday the newspapers are crammed full of opportunities. It is common for younger people starting out to "try out" two or three careers before settling on the one they plan to follow.

MAIRI SEMPLE

The Star Ferry is an icon of Hong Kong. This famous seven minute journey is made approximately 450 times per day.

日理萬城

THE "STAR" FERRY
TO
HONG KONG
CENTRAL, WANCHAI
HARBOUR CRUISES
BOOK INSIDE

MAIRI SEMPLE

A plethora of transport options are at the finger-tips of Hong Kong denizens.

MAIRI SEMPLE

Built in 1904 the Hong Kong Tram line is the oldest and cheapest form of transportation. For less than US$1 a colorful trip on a double decker can take you through 30 kilometres of track which once travelled along the shore of Hong Kong.

PETER DANFORD

HKTA

Jetfoils and Turbo Cats speed out of the Shun Tak terminal. But if you are in a real hurry you could always jump on a helicopter to Macau instead.

BG 7591

From chauffeurs of pink Rolls Royces to cleaners of the visiting QE2, Hong Kong's diligent and dedicated work force is a major contributing factor to its success.

Always in the back of everyone's mind is the ultimate Hong Kong goal: to make it big, to have your own company, your own flat and your own car. Tycoons are envied, but they are also admired and emulated. Hong Kong must be one of the few places on earth where the most respected man in town is also the wealthiest. For many, Li Ka-Shing is the ultimate role model. Whether it is through winning the MarkSix lottery, placing a lucky bet at the Happy Valley horse races, or because of just plain hard work, Hong Kong is characterised by this pervasive "feel good" factor of working hard to succeed.

So what is it that people actually do when they get to work? What kind of an economy does Hong Kong have?

A man on a bicycle transports an important cargo across town, just in time for lunch.

DAVE PARKER

MAIRI SEMPLE

MARTIN BUCKLEY

MARTIN BUCKLEY

The general rhythm of Hong Kong is frenetic, yet all listen to their own tune contributing to the richness of the composition which is Hong Kong.

From a medicinal cup of tea, to dragon's beard candy, or even if it is just a glass of fresh juice: all can be found anywhere on the streets of Hong Kong.

Hong Kong is a true kaleidoscope of images, from five-star restaurants to thirst quenching fruit juice stalls, served with a beaming smile.

Hong Kong is one of
the busiest container
ports in the world.
Approximately
215,000 vessels
arrive each year to
this hub port
strategically located
at the mouth of the
Pearl River.

*With the amount of glass
in the city, there is
always a job for a
window cleaner. But
make sure you get paid
danger money.*

*A butcher in Wan Chai takes
a break to smile at the camera.*

Fishmongers, art dealers, silversmiths, pipe sealers - one of the largest bazaars in the world is at your disposal to investigate and explore.

BAYON PUBLISHING

DVIR BAR-GAL

PETER DANFORD

The Way Things Work

There is one telling statistic that illuminates powerfully this individual, entrepreneurial genius that is Hong Kong at work. There are approximately 100,000 trading companies in Hong Kong, and of these some 98 per cent are small and medium sized enterprises (SMEs). The story of Hong Kong's success is the story of these small companies, often family-owned, which were started by the different waves of people who came to Hong Kong.

Traders from Guangzhou came early in the century, looking for increased business in the West, while refugees fleeing trauma on the mainland came during 1949 and 1950, and again from the mid 1960's to the mid 1970's. Overwhelmingly the people who came to Hong Kong came to trade - to start family businesses and to work to get ahead. Today, these same Hong Kong companies are among the world's most successful and sophisticated small businesses, representing comparatively few industries: garments, electronics, toys, fabrics and promotional items. Some have grown into sizable empires, regional powers in property development (Hutchison Whampoa and Hopewell), clothing (Giordano and Dickson Concepts) and electronics (V-Tech), to name just a few.

But even the smaller ones carry clout. It is estimated that some 40 per cent of these 100,000 trading companies have operations in two or more countries. It is these small companies that form the economic backbone of Hong Kong, though they are not alone.

One of the interesting things about Hong Kong's economy is that it is dominated by companies on either end of the size spectrum. If the soul of Hong Kong is the small, family-owned business, the glamour is provided by the huge *hongs*, which grew up over the years and now have dealings in virtually every facet of Hong Kong's economy. Lately, the original *hongs* of Hong Kong - great trading and financial companies like Jardine's and Swire - have been joined by massive enterprises from the mainland like CITIC, the investment arm of the mainland government.

Pots, pans, tubes, pipes and yarn, are all for sale.

Far Left: Umbrellas are a necessity in Hong Kong, where average rainfall can reach 400mm a month.

Left: What may seem to be 'lap-sap' (rubbish) to some, is a tradable commodity to others.

In addition to the small companies and the *hongs* there is also a third major player in Hong Kong's economy: the multinationals. There are some 2,000 multinationals at work in Hong Kong and this greatly contributes to Hong Kong's international character. Most of the companies tend to be in either finance or the service sector. Hong Kong has an exceptionally strong confluence of service sector companies, everything from telecommunications and advertising to transportation and architecture, making it Asia's service hub.

Taken together, the SMEs, the *hongs*, and the multinationals have contributed to Hong Kong's status as one of the four Asian "tiger" economies. Hong Kong currently ranks as the world's seventh largest trading economy and ninth largest exporter of services. Hong Kong's GDP was an impressive US$153 billion in 1996 and per capita income is rocketing up. At more than US$24,000 in 1996, Hong Kong is wealthier on a per capita basis than most West European countries. Inflation is a manageable six per cent and unemployment remains under three per cent. The growth rate is still a robust 5.5 per cent.

There are some broad patterns of work in Hong Kong. More and more the financial day operates round the clock, as Hong Kong has moved alongside Tokyo as a twin financial centre of Asia. With London and New York on-line, the dealmaking never really stops. In addition, Hong Kong traders have almost two decades worth of experience dealing with the China market, sourcing products and supervising production. Travel back and forth between Hong Kong and China is increasing, as is Hong Kong's participation in mainland projects. Finally, Hong Kong business people find themselves doing business around the region with fully one third of trade taking place within Asia. The other two thirds of trade is split evenly between the West and China.

Change of sovereignty in Hong Kong affected the status of a number of British nationals.

At the onset of the 21st century, Hong Kong is well positioned to take advantage of further growth in the region. The unique combination of powerful *hongs*, international companies and small, home-grown businesses has given Hong Kong's economy a overall dynamism that matches the spirit of the working individual.

Hong Kong boasts the largest number of mobile phones per capita in the world. Where space is a commodity and time is money the ease of communication is crucial.

The Shape of Things to Come

In 1979, the year Deng Xiaoping opened southern China to market reform and established the special economic zones, Hong Kong's economy was in the middle of a major structural change. Hong Kong had been a trading entrepôt and a manufacturing centre but by 1979 about 64 per cent of Hong Kong's GDP came from services. Eighteen years later that figure is 85 per cent and Hong Kong has become the world's most service-oriented economy.

Even anecdotal evidence would suggest that. At countless taxi stands around the city on a Friday night, the talk is of where different executives will be the following week. An engineering specialist is going to Manila for talks on an infrastructure joint venture. An advertising executive is flying to Shanghai to pitch the latest strategy for his client's rapidly expanding brand in China. A banker is flying to Kuala Lumpur to offer a training course on a new treasury management system developed in Hong Kong.

Quietly but quickly, Hong Kong has become Asia's services hub - the nerve centre of an expanding and more prosperous regional economy.

In the years to come, it is likely that more and more manufacturing will leave Hong Kong for cheaper locales and that, like New York and London, Hong Kong will become the value-added, service support centre for the surrounding economy. Particularly in China, Hong Kong business people will find themselves flying to an ever-increasing number of destinations to provide expertise to all manner of projects.

MICHAEL CHUNG

MARK PRESLEY

There is a vast array of budding talent in the Hong Kong fashion and film scene. The creative arts have blossomed internationally, gaining a new reputation around the globe.

*On location in
the New Territories
for the filming of
an international
television commercial.*

DVIR BAR-GAL

MARK BUCKLEY

Above: *The firing of Hong Kong's Noon Day Gun in Causeway Bay is a regular daily spectacle.*

Right: *Nepalese Ex-Ghurkas are still employed in Hong Kong often in security positions.*

Working in the lifts of some of the tallest buildings in the world.

MARTIN BUCKLEY

In addition to its role as a service hub for Asia, Hong Kong is wielding an increasing amount of financial clout with 82 of the world's 100 largest banks located here. Since 1993 Hong Kong has been the world's 4th leading source of foreign direct investment ahead of Japan and France, first in the ASEAN group of countries and first in APEC. Some of the money is raised locally, principally through the large property and project developers in Hong Kong. However, much of the money is being channelled through Hong Kong by the overseas Chinese network, Western companies and investors eager to be part of the economic growth and opportunities in the next 25 years.

What this means for Hong Kong is a tremendous amount of influence and a great deal of work funding and supporting projects around the region and especially in China. The China connection will obviously grow stronger. Red chip stocks have for awhile been among the best performing stocks on the Hong Kong Exchange. More and more former state-owned enterprises are coming to Hong Kong to list publicly on the exchange, to gain expertise and to make contacts with Western financial markets. More Hong Kong people are being employed on the mainland, again offering expertise and training in areas like accounting, project management and hotels, and there will also be a far greater number of mainland businessmen who will come to Hong Kong to make deals.

What this all adds up to is something of a new role for Hong Kong - something not seen in Asia before. Sort of a supermarket for the region. The place where ideas are generated, projects are co-ordinated and deals are done. The place where, despite all the money and the multinationals - it is still the power of the individual, the entrepreneurial genius of Hong Kong, that is the strongest and most lasting aspect of this city at work.

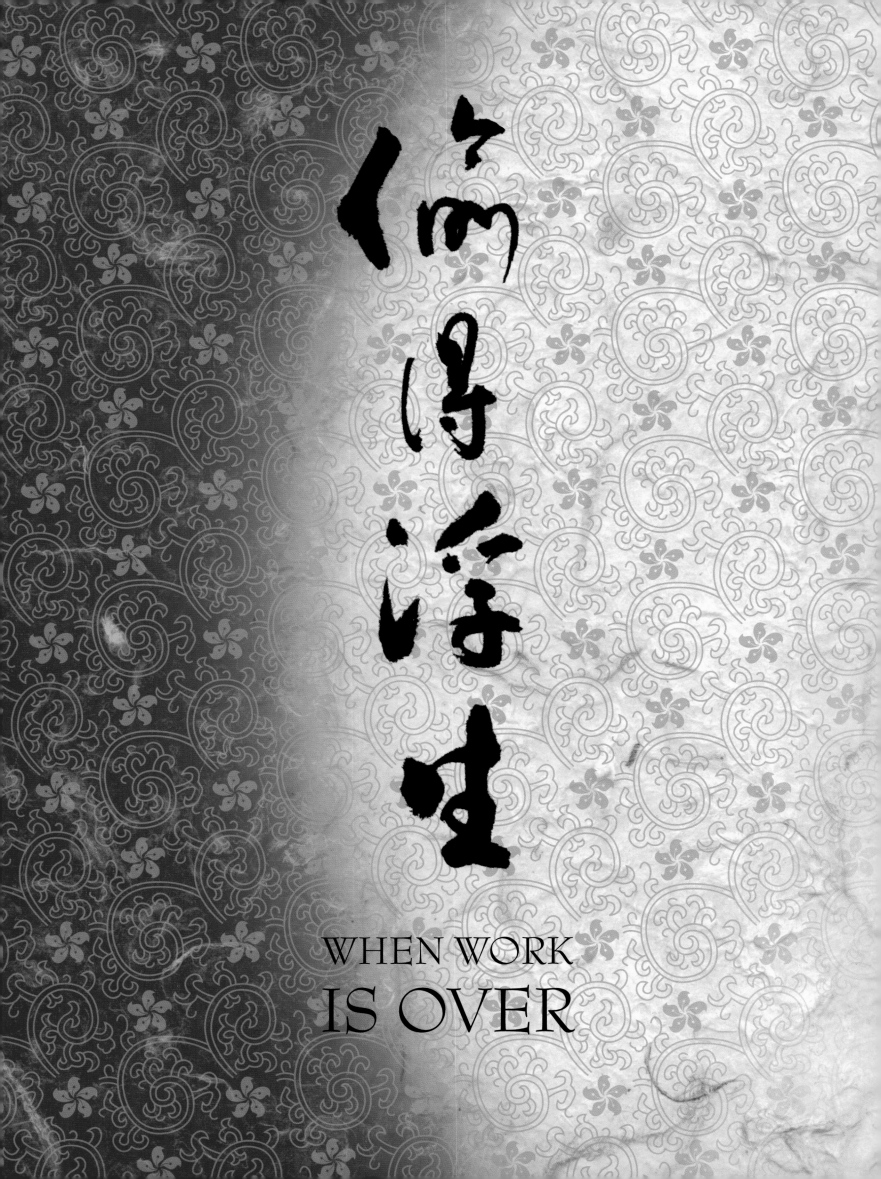

偷得浮生

WHEN WORK
IS OVER

New Casual Styling

PETER DANFORD

MARTIN BUCKLEY

PETER DANFORD

After Hours

by Vivien Jones

Hong Kong is a city where native Hakka and Hoklo people still live traditional lives on the sea, where tycoons, many as rich as some small countries, build extravagant mansions on some of the priciest real estate on the planet, where a two-bedroomed apartment can command in excess of US$2 million and a 'lucky' license plate costs more than the car. Where the standard of living outstrips that of Britain, Germany and Canada, and the tax rates are among the lowest in the world. People from every corner of the globe are drawn to Hong Kong to make their fortunes and end up making it their home as well. A cosmopolitan city with few equals, Hong Kong is a city of superlatives. You could dine at a different restaurant every night of the year in Hong Kong and still not exhaust the possibilities. One restaurant for every 650 people means a lot of choice. They drink more cognac here than anywhere else in the world, wager more money on the horses (one in six people place bets every race day, spending an estimated US$1,690 for every man, woman and child), and, surprisingly, have one of the longest life expectancies (second only to sleepy San Marino). Hong Kong has the world's biggest neon sign (the 999 Nanfang Pharmaceutical factory takes that honour), the most Rolls Royces per capita, the highest concentration of cellular phones, and the largest outdoor seated Buddha, gazing benevolently over Lantau.

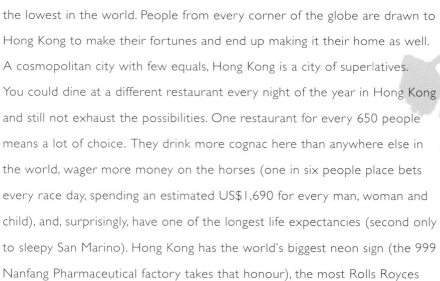

PETER DANFORD

A single serving of abalone can cost US$2,600 and snake soup is a winter favourite for its supposed aphrodisiac qualities. In the markets of Central and Wanchai, early morning shoppers haggle loudly over leafy piles of *pak choi* and *choi sum*. Stalls are heaped high with baskets of bean sprouts and straw mushrooms fresh from China and the New Territories, live chickens blink blankly from wicker cages fish and frogs are summarily delivered to the chopping block.

The sights and sounds of Hong Kong insistently overwhelm the senses. By day, the trill of song fills the lanes of the Bird Market where row upon row of teak cages shelter exotic birds of every ilk, and a feathered friend can set you back US$2,000. By night, Temple Street in Kowloon is transformed into a hurly-burly of fortune tellers, CD sellers, *dai pai dongs*, and opera singers. In Kowloon's Jade Market, business is a mix of hard-headed practicality and secret symbolism. Negotiations are conducted through a series of mysterious hand signals in an exchange that leaves only the buyer and seller privy to the final price.

For all its reputation as a city of workaholics, Hong Kong has ample opportunity for play. Amidst the hustle and bustle, nearly 40 per cent of the land is set aside as country parks. Granite and volcanic mountains, formed 160 million years ago, are crisscrossed with tracks and trails and fringed with white sandy beaches. Despite the constant development, some have made Hong Kong's wilder reaches home: the Romer's Tree Frog is an exclusive resident in this region as are the much-threatened pink dolphins, only 80 of which remain in the waters north of Lantau. The Mai Po Nature Reserve in the New Territories plays host to 325 species of birds each year, including the Asiatic golden plover and the black tailed godwit who stop over to dine at the reserve's shrimp ponds.

Corporate 'splat ball' or relaxing on the company junk is a welcome relief to the rigours of a six day working week.

This business executive takes time out during his lunch break enjoying his favourite past time.

*Careening along!
This rollercoaster
is one of the more
exhilarating rides
at Ocean Park.*

As night falls on Shatin Racecourse the crowds eagerly wait for the evening races on the floodlit track to begin.

History of Hong Kong Racing

by Z. Greenstreet Kan

Hong Kong horseracing first started with the Gymkhana. Nowadays, few people know what a Gymkhana is all about. When the British Empire was at its peak, officers in various branches of His or Her Majesty's military services brought different types of equestrian skills to all corners of the world, and Gymkhana is the all embracing word for sports that involving horses are teamed up with different sportsmen.

Once the British had established their footings in Hong Kong, one form or another of horseracing was organised by military personnel. It was still the age of Hussars, Lancers and Dragoons, so most officers were very familiar with war-horses. When there was no war on the horizon, war-horses became the natural source of matching speed, and from there it was just a short leap to having racing meetings staged.

Close to thirty years elapsed before the British populace felt it appropriate to form organised horseracing, and that was how the Hong Kong Jockey Club was founded. Garrison troops were still the mainstay, but civilian riders, used to foxhunts and point-to-point racing in their homeland, started to make their presence felt.

It was the time when treaty ports abounded all along the coast, so the development of organised horseracing was not confined to Hong Kong alone. Tientsin (now Tianjin), Shanghai, Tsingtao (now Qingdao), Hankow (now part of Wuhan) were among the more prominent centres of racing along with Hong Kong.

At that period of time, horseracing was still essentially treated as a sport, and its "by-product" of wagering on the results was taken only lightly. It remained an amateur sport for a long time. Jockeys were true "gentlemen riders" in those days, with a fair number of them actually owning the horses that they rode.

Horses were motley groups, haphazardly assembled from many different sources. Not until the turn of the century did China ponies (in fact they came from Outer Mongolia) dominate the scene. A steady supply route was set. Horse dealers brought in hundreds through a well-known Great Wall station-gate called Zhangjiakao and had their first stop in Tientsin. There, once the major owners had their first pick, they were shipped through

the ancient canal headed for Shanghai. By the time the owners once again made their selections the remaining horses would head south first touching Amoy (now Xiamen) and spend the last leg of their journey to Hong Kong by ship.

By the early thirties, the inevitable Sino-Japanese war was imminent and the supply route of China ponies was stopped. Walers from Australia were shipped in to fill the void. Because the speed of Walers and China ponies differed to a tremendous extent, Hong Kong racing during the 1930's and the early 1940's consisted of a two-tiered system: half of the races were for China ponies and the other half for the Australian ponies, the two never meeting in any race.

Each horse has its own special diet of oats, meal and vitamins.

Shredded paper is used in each horse's stall. Although it is a little more expensive than straw it does not create dust which can irritate the temperamental racehorses.

The trainers watch the progress of their horses during the early morning track work.

Prizes are often given for the best turned-out horse in the parade ring. The crowds look on in anticipation for their favourite as they wait for the next race.

At the outbreak of the Pacific War Hong Kong fell to the invading Japanese and was under Military occupation for more than three and a half years. Nevertheless during that period of time races were being held every two weeks until almost the end of the war. Having no new replacements, the horse population dwindled to a mere fifty or fewer towards the end of this period. In order to frame enough horses for a meeting, certain races were reduced to distance handicapping events or mounted trots. As a last resort, half of the programme would use wooden horses on sliding strings to satisfy those who still cared to gamble on the outcome of such farcical events.

Above: *Bagpipes entertain the crowd. Racing can be a fun day out for all the family.*

Middle Right and Bottom Right: *Millions of dollars are gambled on every race on the card. In Hong Kong there are both on-track and off-track betting facilities, so anyone can have a flutter.*

Following the form and a little bit of luck is the recipe for a happy day at the races. In Hong Kong racing is easily the most popular spectator sport.

Racing during the Japanese occupation might not have amounted to much, but it did have its merits. The most significant contribution was the introduction of Chinese text with everything that went with racing. Previously, no official Chinese translation of any kind existed where horseracing was concerned. Since then the names of have been in two languages and have become standardised. Formerly horseracing had been a sport for elitists only and had not catered for the "hoi polloi" who did not speak or read English. All of a sudden it became much more accessible and many people believe that, to a tremendous extent, it was that factor alone that helped popularise horseracing in Hong Kong.

The stands are packed full right up to the rail, with everyone craning their neck to get a better view.

Right: *And they're off!!*

Getting back to the beginning of the Jockey Club, no Chinese were admitted in its membership prior to the 1920's. Segregated wood and bamboo pavilions were erected quite a distance from the stands that housed the Taipans and assorted Caucasians. Therefore the tragic fire that happened on Derby Day in 1918 in Happy Valley did not affect a single "Gweilo" (foreigner) while more than six hundred Chinese perished because they were segregated into different stands.

The Great Strike of 1925 had paralysed Hong Kong and many Chinese workers had returned to Canton (now Guangzhou) because the political climate at that point in history fueled a strong sense of xenophobia. A few leading compradores used their power of persuasion to successfully drag those workers back to Hong Kong and everything was back to normal before long. As a token of appreciation to those compradores, the jockey club opened its doors to Chinese members, and the rest, as they say, is history.

Although World War II ended in August 1945 and the British resumed administration of Hong Kong in September, the Jockey Club did not become operational again until early 1947. Between September 1945 and January 1947, race meetings were held first in Fanling and then in Happy Valley, but only military horses were used, and the riders came from the ranks and files of the British forces.

A batch of ninety Walers were again shipped to Hong Kong from Australia in the autumn of 1946 to prepare for the 1947 resumption of club racing; but the Jockey Club found it hard to find enough members subscribing for the ponies. Most would-be owners were persuaded to take more than one pony in that batch. The most supportive was T.K. Lee who claimed five and named them in alphabetical order; those five being Annatola, Betty Lou, Cassie, Daisy Bell and Elmer. From the 1950's onward, over-subscription became the norm and some owners would have to try five or six times in consecutive years before landing the right to own one pony. Telling them that not long ago T.K.Lee had the 'luck' of landing five in one year became a difficult story to believe.

Happy Valley was essentially built for ponies, but by the 1960's it became apparent that ponies were hard to come by and the Jockey Club had to remedy the situation by allowing the importation of horses instead.

Betting volumes started to improve from year to year during the 1950's and 1960's and by the mid 1960's, illegal bookmaking became prevalent. With the setup of amateur horseracing it was hard to stamp out such unlawful dealings. Big bookmakers tried to tamper with the natural results of racing, and in doing so, more than half of the horses in the active list were found to have been doped on numerous different occasions.

In a blur of colour the horses flash past the grandstand at Shatin on their way to the winning post. The noise of the crowd rises as the line approaches.

*An army of
workers replace
the divots on the
track in between
each race.*

*The sun sets on an evening
meeting at Happy Valley
Racecourse. Surrounded by
commercial and residential
skyscrapers this is one of
the most spectacular inner
city tracks in the world.*

By the beginning of the 1970's, the situation was getting out of control and the Jockey Club finally decided to do away with amateur racing and turn to fully-fledged professionalism. The new era dawned in the autumn of 1971. Just half a year earlier the club had also decided to import nothing other than thoroughbreds in succeeding replacement batches of horses. The first ones came from Australia and New Zealand, but within a decade had broadened bases of supply from Great Britain, Ireland, France, the United States and Canada. Occasionally even Swedish-bred, Argentine-bred and Indian-bred horses were also imported.

Professional racing meant much tighter control on stable security. It also meant that jockeys were given a much stricter code of on-course as well as off-course behaviour. Professional racing enabled the Club to turn international in many aspects of the game. First it joined the Asian Racing Conference as a member "nation" and then it staged international races for world-renowned jockeys to grace the scene.

By the mid 1970's it became apparent that Hong Kong would need a new racecourse in addition to Happy Valley, and the blueprint for Shatin was created. To level a few hilltops and use the landfill to reclaim part of a bay was a mammoth task, but the Jockey Club turned that dream into reality in record time. Shatin started racing in the latter part of 1978.

By the 1980's, the Jockey Club launched another ambitious project by staging International races. This involved inviting horses from abroad to compete with local champions and within a few years the number of these races rose from one to four each season. Such a mode of invitational was started by the United States' Washington D.C. International at Laurel, Maryland. Horses invited would not have to pay an entry fee.

MAIRI SEMPLE

The cost of the two-way transportation as well as their owners, jockeys, trainers and grooms was covered by the Club and every expense was taken care of. All were regarded as guests at these prestigious events and this demonstrated to the world that Hong Kong racing had really come of age.

At the end of the 1980's, with advanced technology in satellite transmission, Hong Kong also began to have simulcasts of the world's major horseracing events. Soon it became a "two-way street", as more and more Hong Kong immigrants settled in North America.

A trainer's work is never done. Australian David Hayes, one of Hong Kong's leading trainers, discusses his prospects with an eager news team.

They were able to continue to support Hong Kong racing by following the goings-on and in fact betting more heavily on independent pools in Canada and the United States than races staged in those simulcast sites. For the new 1997/98 season, Hong Kong racing is being followed at racetracks in over five U.S. states (California, Massachusetts, Ohio, Texas and New Jersey) and six Canadian provinces (British Columbia, Ontario, Quebec, Manitoba, Alberta and Saskatchewan).

Betting-wise, Hong Kong racing is well known for its exciting variety of "exotic" bets. Place Quinella, Tierce, Interlocking Doubles, Trebles, Six-Up, Double Trio, Triple Trio, you name it, they have got it. The hugely successful Triple Trio attracted television crews from more than twenty countries in the final meeting before the sovereignty changeover because in that particular pool a mind-boggling sum of close to $700 million was wagered, a figure that will surely end up in the Guinness Book of Records.

From Gymkhana to the Guinness Book of Records, Hong Kong's horseracing has indeed had an amazing growth that begs comparison. As to what the future holds, the sky is the limit and there's no buts about it.

*World Number one
Pete Sampras and
Hong Kong's favourite
Michael Chang
regularly play in tennis
events in Victoria Park.
Table tennis is also
popular in the Region.*

Left: *Imported sand is used to make a beach volleyball court for the International Beach Volleyball event.*

Bottom left: *Chelsea, 1997 English FA Cup winners, walk onto the pitch alongside local team South China. Hong Kong has hosted such teams as Inter Milan and Manchester United.*

Rock climbing is available for the braver sportsmen. Sailing and recently windsurfing are also very popular. Lee Lai-shan can be seen in action. She is Hong Kong's only Olympic Gold medal winner.

CHRIS COURT

OOCL

HKTA

If the pressure of work is really getting to you why not jump out of a plane !

CHRIS COURT

拳世嬌回

THE WORLD

WAS WATCHING

and dignitaries on July 1st, 1997.

A new sight in Hong Kong. An immaculately dressed sentry from the People's Liberation Army stands guard outside the Prince of Wales Barracks in Admiralty district.

The first members of the PLA arrive over the border at Lok Ma Lhau. This is the first time the PLA has set foot on Hong Kong territory.

The world's press turned out to witness this historic event.

MAIRI SEMPLE

DVIR BAR GAL

British TV presenter Trevor McDonald was one of the many who decended on Hong Kong to get the scoop.

DAVE PARKER

Hong Kong becomes a splash of light and colour with posters announcing a 'Unity' party.

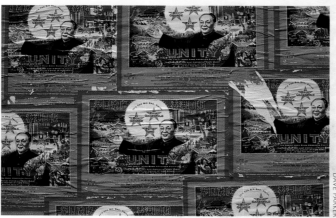

Eclectic and unique souvenirs in every imaginable shape and form were marketed .

DVIR BAR. GAL

In the sound bites that were beamed live around the world on the momentous change of sovereignty, Hong Kong was called many things. For the 6.4 million residents who woke up in the new SAR on July 1st, it is above all home. In the words of the Chief Executive, Hong Kong people are finally the masters of their own house.

In thirty-six hours that went around the globe, the world turned to gaze on a small island, glittering brightly in the South China Seas. Midnight, June 30th, 1997: Hong Kong's date with destiny had been anticipated for more than a decade and it was clear, as this paragon of capitalism returned to the embrace of a communist motherland, that it was to be a date of momentous importance. Rarely before had one power surrendered such a rich and valuable prize to another.

Above: The last Governor of Hong Kong, Mr Chris Patten, receives the British flag at the Governors Residence.

Right: The old red colonial post boxes were removed to make way for new bright green ones.

A borrowed city living on borrowed time, Hong Kong's history has always been indelibly linked to that of the mainland. Colonised as a conduit for British opium trade with China, there were just 5,000 residents when the British raised the flag at Possession Point, 2,000 of whom were fishermen living on the sea. Today, 6.4 million people live and work in Hong Kong, many of them descendants of successive waves of refugees and immigrants seeking sanctuary from the tumult of the communist mainland. The waves of China

SINOPIX

Choreographed dances performed by children during the Tamar ceremony.

have always lapped at Hong Kong's shores and there remains a symbiotic relationship - culturally and economically - between the two. The moment of their reunion was headline-grabbing stuff.

Eight thousand accredited journalists (and many more unofficial ones) descended on the territory to chronicle an event that had all the ingredients of a great story: was the End of an Empire, A New Era, the Dawn of a New Dynasty. What is more, it was one of the most exciting and dynamic cities in the world, an international dynamo set to return to the world's largest communist state.

In the days leading up to the handover, Hong Kong took a holiday - an unprecedented five days in a city of workaholics. Bars and restaurants overflowed with revelers and the streets were crowded with shoppers snapping up handover souvenirs that ranged from the benign to the ridiculous. Stamps bearing the Queen's head were a hot investment property, causing queues that stretched for hours. A rash of watches, pens, lighters and paperweights hit the streets and T-shirts bearing the legend 'Hong Kong: The Great Chinese Take Away' were a humorous take on the proceedings. Canned colonial air proved a last minute favourite among Hong Kongers eager to mark the event the best way they knew how: shopping.

Mr Chris Patten makes his final and somewhat emotional speech to the crowd at the Tamar site. British dignitaries look on with umbrellas as the final hours of the British Colonisation of Hong Kong come to an end.

Over two rain-soaked nights, nearly 50 tonnes of explosives were let loose in Hong Kong's skies. Nearly half a million people watched the last British display of pyrotechnics, which was followed the next evening by a laser extravaganza put on by China that used more sound and light equipment than any show ever before.

Not even a failed attempt to capture the world karaoke record could dampen spirits on that night. The famous Hong Kong skyline was wallpapered with neon: pink dolphins and dragons frolicked across skyscrapers draped with the symbol of the new SAR, the bauhinia flower.

Ten thousand pigeons from as far away as the northern Chinese province of Xinjiang were released in the territory to symbolise Hong Kong's return to the motherland, and across Hong Kong parties were held to mark the auspicious event. In Happy Valley, the world's hottest Canto pop stars danced and sang in a performance that reflected the energy of this cosmopolitan city. Against a dramatic backdrop of the island's skyline, Chinese American Yo-Yo Ma and Beijing-born composer Tan Dun performed Tan's hour-long '1997 Symphony - Heaven Earth Man', accompanied by orchestra, cello, traditional brass bells and a 300-voice children's choir.

On the mainland, a hundred thousand people gathered before a giant countdown clock in Tiananmen Square, dancing and singing until the early hours of the morning when the Chinese flag was first raised in Hong Kong. Similar scenes were played out in Shanghai, Tianjin, Guangzhou and Shenzhen, and gifts flooded into

AFP

*The Union Jack
flag and the
Hong Kong flag
are lowered amidst
emotional scenes
at the Tamar Site
as the Band of the
Black Watch play
the 'Last Post'.*

Hong Kong from every province and region of China, including a six metre high bronze and gold plated sculpture from the central government. In the Beijing Workers Stadium, 18,000 performers reenacted scenes from Chinese history for assembled dignitaries. Among them, President Jiang Zemin who the day before had become the first Chinese head of state ever to set foot on Hong Kong soil.

From the moment the last governor of Hong Kong left Government House, carrying out the traditional three turns around the drive to signify that he would return, it was evident it would be a day of equal part cheers and tears. Battling torrential rains, 10,000 people attended a British farewell ceremony at HMS Tamar that included a performance by children dressed as stockbrokers brandishing cellular phones.

Quintessential Hong Kong.

In the New Territories, members of the Tang clan, one of Hong Kong's oldest, gathered in the family's 700 year old ancestral hall to celebrate the handover, while at the ultra-expensive Regent Hotel guests partied at an event that called for colonial attire before midnight and Chinese thereafter.

The Tamar Site: the June 30th multimillion dollar fireworks extravaganza sponsored by ING Barings.
Two gigantic screens broadcast the ceremonies around the globe.

In a dignified ceremony in the extension of the New Convention and Exhibition Centre, the red and gold flag of the Peoples Republic of China flies high alongside the new bauhinia flag of Hong Kong

DAVID G. McINTYRE

The President of China, Mr. Jiang Zemin
in a handshake with His Royal Highness
Prince Charles, The Prince of Wales.
Jiang Zemin is the first Head of State
to set foot in the territory.

紅旗飄揚

Meanwhile the party continues but now it is China's party.

Above: *In the early hours of the morning of July 1st, at the new Convention and Exhibition Centre, Mr. Tung Chee-hwa swears in the new Legislative Council led by the provisional legislature President Rita Fan Hsu Lai-Tai.*

Right: *The Hong Kong Philharmonic Orchestra play a moving piece to celebrate the handover with traditional brass bells. The 1997 symphony "Heaven Earth Mankind" was composed by Beijing born Tan Dun and Chinese-American Yo-Yo Ma. The bells were a replica of a set discovered in a tomb which dates back between 475BC and 221BC in Hubei province.*

*Mr. Tung Chee-hwa
presides over the start of
the second fireworks
spectacular as the aptly
named "Pearl of the
Orient" show begins.*

EDWIN TUVAY

MAIRI SEMPLE

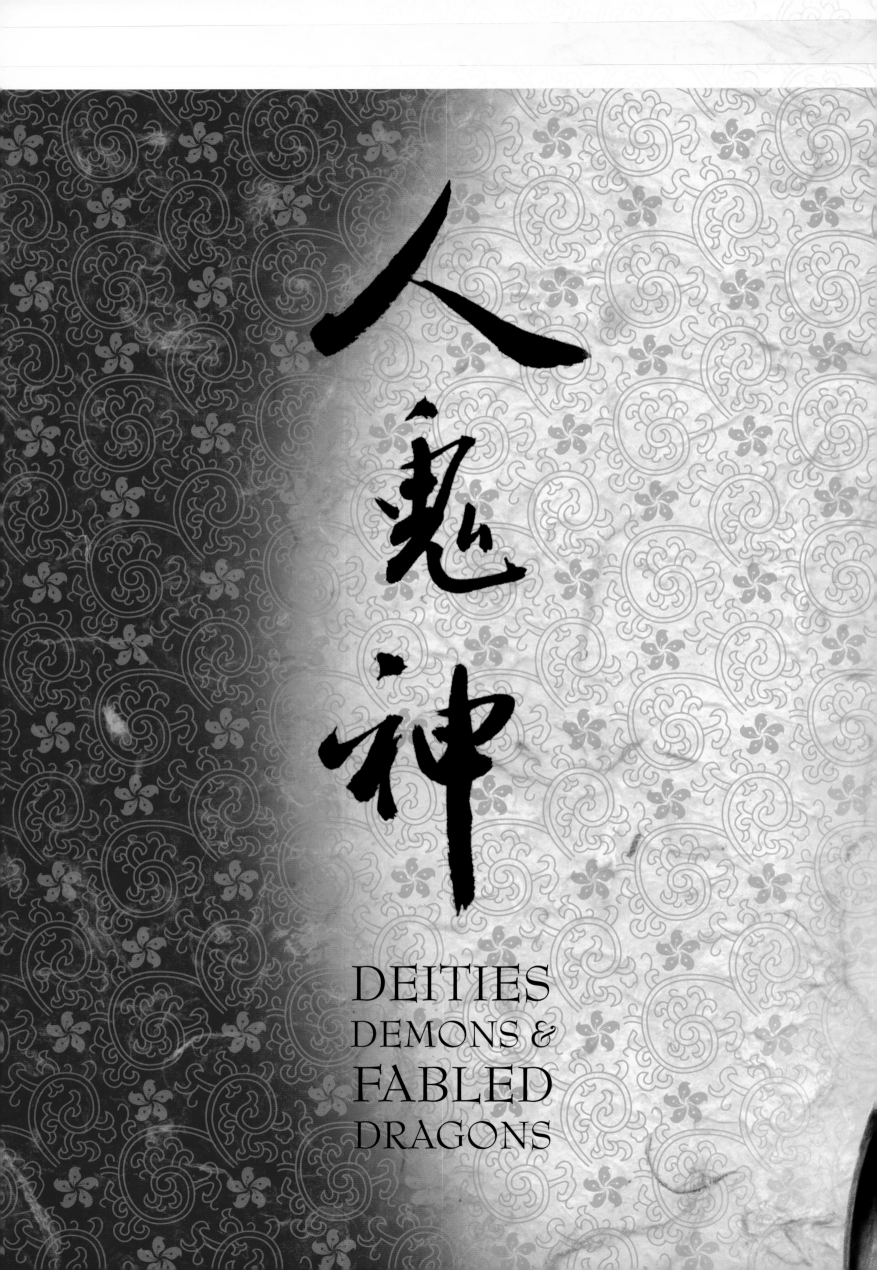

人鬼神

DEITIES
DEMONS &
FABLED
DRAGONS

*Dazzling New Year's
Fireworks illuminate
Hong Kong's
impressive Victoria
Harbour. Celebration
of the Lunar New Year
Festival is a 4,000
year old ritual which
lasts for two weeks.*

*A Hakka woman
tends to her
precious plum tree
which symbolises
good luck in the
forthcoming year.*

HKTA

*"May you have a
happy and prosperous
New Year". The God
of riches presides over
its devotees bringing
them wealth, good
fortune and longevity.*

MICHEL PORRO

KUNG HEI FAT CHOY

Oranges are harbingers of good luck and are often eaten throughout the Lunar New Year Festival. During this time multitudes of tangerine trees adorn the offices and restaurants in Hong Kong.

The Lunar New Year Festival is a family-oriented celebration, whereupon children and unmarried friends receive red packets of lai see - or lucky money.

MAIRI SEMPLE

Children represent the innocence of the holy sage, absorbing all that it sees. Chinese festivals are colourful events and encourage people of all ages to participate.

A woman on a float waves her bouquet to the crowds at the Chinese New Year Parade.

MAIRI SEMPLE

PASCALE SYSTERMANS

人
鬼
神

The Cheung Chau Bun festival is unique to Hong Kong. It is a festival celebrated to mollify the spirits of the dead.

PASCALE SYSTERMANS

Young children are dressed as historical figures on ingeniously wired "floating" frames as they participate in the procession throughout the village.

Ornately dressed men, costumed in various traditional garments, enter into the spirit of the parade.

Musical instruments are used to express the harmony between heaven and earth.

*A young boy picks
out his favorite
lantern.*

MARTIN BUCKLEY

The Mid-Autumn festival celebrates the ripening harvest with mooncakes and lanterns. Victoria Park has become a favorite venue for these gatherings.

DVIR BAR-GAL

MAIRI SEMPLE

HKTA

Lanterns are symbols of illumination and knowledge. Predominately paper or cotton cloth lanterns were hung to guide the souls of ancestors back to the other world.

MAIRI SEMPLE

MAIRI SEMPLE

Mountains of edible buns tower the bamboo scaffolding of the Cheung Chau celebrations. Traditionally whoever scrambles to the top and retrieves the highest bun wins the highest honour.

HKTA

Dragon Dancing: the colourful hues and eloquent movements of the dance fascinate the spectators. Dragons are complex multi-tiered symbols of male vigour and fertility as well as being a symbol of the East.

Tin Hau pennants carry messages of peace and blessings to the Goddess, Tin Hau, who protects the fisherfolk, bringing them good fortune.

*Flags line the piers of
outlying islands.
Boats and Gods in
miniature adorn the
sculptures which are
carried on procession
throughout the town.*

The many faces of Chinese opera

All photographs by Pascale Systermans

MAIRI SEMPLE

MAIRI SEMPLE

Burning incense or joss sticks is an integral part of worship to various deities in the Buddhist faith.

Buddhist monks make the trek to Tiantan Buddha situated on Lantau Island. This forty metre high Buddha is the largest outdoor seated Buddha in the world.

In Chinese, xiang (incense) means fragrance. These sandalwood scented sticks come in various sizes and coil shapes.

PAUL HILTON

PAUL HILTON

PAUL HILTON

MICHEL PORRO

The Tai Ping Ching Djiu Festival occurs only once every ten years. Spectators watch as the massive effigy is engulfed in the conflagration.

市的桃源

BEYOND THE
SKYSCRAPERS

With all the rush and stress of the big city, people sometimes take for granted the natural beauty which surrounds the region, making it such a unique area.

*Children are
the future of
Hong Kong.
They will grow
into adults in a
region that can
control its own
destiny.*

Tai O in Lantau Island offers an alternative to the hustle and bustle of the Metropolis.

HONG KONG - DAWN OF A NEW DYNASTY

In an archipelago of over 200 islands, boats are the more frequent form of transport. Scenic fishing villages dot many of the Outlying Islands.

MAIRI SEMPLE

HKTA

HKTA

With the amount of building going on sand carrying barges will never be idle.

MAIRI SEMPLE

HONG KONG · DAWN OF A NEW DYNASTY

*An old lady chops
and cleans the
catch of the day by
the seashore.*

*The ancestors of the
Hakka Farmers and the
Tanka and Hoklo
fisherfolk are still to be
found in the outlying
islands. These indigenous
people were the first
inhabitants of Hong Kong
and their origins go back
to Neolithic times.*

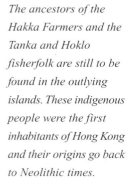

Some of the old colonial style buildings can still be seen in the Outlying Islands. It is possible to create an understanding of how the region used to look in days past as this type of building was bulldozed long ago to make way for the skyscrapers seen today.

For many generations day to day life remains the same in the pressure free rural regions.

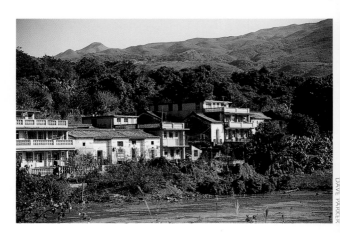

Sai Kung is one part of Hong Kong that retains its natural beauty. The area at the northern most part of the New Territories is a National Park with the famous Maclehose Trail cutting through it. If you are prepared to walk, deserted beaches can be found.

MARTIN BUCKLEY

MAIRI SEMPLE

MARTIN BUCKLEY

It is possible to find alternatives to the high-rise blocks of the city centre.

MARK PRESLEY

Hong Kong is more than just a "Barren Rock" but there are still a few to be seen in the far flung regions. This is the High Island Reservoir in the Sai Kung East Country Park.

MARTIN BUCKLEY

DAVE PARKER

Above:Over 250 species of migratory birds visit Hong Kong, predominately in the Spring and Autumn.

MAIRI SEMPLE

Breathtaking views along the Maclehose trail which spans the new territories, passing through Tai Mo Shan the highest peak in Hong Kong at 957meters.

The border between Hong Kong's New Territories is the dividing line between this Special Administrative Region and the People's Republic of China. Shenzhen can be seen in the distance and is rapidly expanding due to its business ties with Hong Kong.

From the country to the city
Hong Kong is all about
building. Building for the
future, creating new
beginnings and new hope for
all. Opening doors for the
world to come together in
both work and play.